LOGOCRACY

DAILY IMPROVEMENT THROUGH WORDS

2022 WORD JOURNAL

BEN MITCHELL

Logocracy: The Government or rule of words
Adj: [Log-ock-rah-cee]

As we look back through the lens of time a trend of rule is evident. There have been many autocracies (one person with absolute power), lasting ethnocracies (government by one ethnic group for their own gain) and countless kakistocracies (government by the least suitable people). Colonial xenocracies (government by foreign forces), bloody chirocracies (government by physical force) and many unequal androcracies (government by men alone). These eclectic periods of rule pass with time, repeating themselves elsewhere, or never to be seen again. However, there is one form of government that is close to eternal, outlasting the rest. Dictated by one person yet owned by all, this way of rule presides over each of us whilst we preside over it ourselves. It is, the logocracy, the rule or government by words.

Everything begins with a word

*'In the beginning was the Word, and the Word was
with God, and the Word was God'*

John 1:1-14

This excerpt from the Bible is a wonderful place to start when
it comes to proving the existence of the 'Logocracy'. Choosing
to look beyond our religious opinions, we begin to realise the
integral role of words in our lives. Whatever 'God' is to you, it
is defined by a word, Dia (Irish), Gott (German), Allah (Islam)
amongst so many other worshipped deities whose existence
begins with a word. Our world is defined by words, our reality
is defined by and consists of words, they are the architects of
our perception.Take a look around you, notice how you
perceive things, pick one object, notice how you first identify
that object. Take for instance, a yellow flower, it is not the
yellow nature of the flower that we recognize first, but its
essence, its ipseity (individual identity) as a flower. Hence,
words are the gatekeepers to the mind, they bridge the gap
between us and the world. It is clear, then, that words have an
undeniable power of rule over the world, hence the history
thereof.

Moments are defined by words

'Ní briathar a dhearbhaíos ach gníomh'

Above is an old Irish seanfhocal or proverb which translates directly to 'it is not words that affirm but actions'. This old Irish proverb is akin to that of its English counterpart 'Actions speak louder than words' which is recognisable in the form of the popular lyric from the song 'Show me Love' by Robin S. Perhaps it is, amongst other things, the repetition of this statement which has led us to believe in an absolutely independent omnipotence associated with actions. There is no doubt that our actions are far more important than our words, (and we ought not to hide behind or live by our words alone). I do believe, however, that words are given far less credit than they are due. Akin to the age old 'what came first the chicken or the egg' debate, we must wonder, what came first, the word or the thought? I believe that the word comes first. Hence, words precede thought, therefore, action. So actions may speak louder than words but they would also struggle without them.

Owing to this, words also define moments in history. Take for instance, the Moon Landing of July 20th 1969. The echoing words of Neil Armstrong reverberate through time, known verbatim worldwide, they are still recited today.

'That's one small step for man, one giant leap for mankind'

From a similar period in history we look to Martin Luther King Jr, an eloquent civil rights activist who will be remembered for his courage and conduct in fighting against racial segregation. His famous 'I have a dream' speech was a wonderful piece of oratory spoken during the March on Washington of August 28th 1963. Martin Luther Kings' words on that day, and countless other days, transcend his own existence, still surviving and inspiring us today.

> *"I have a dream that one day right down in Alabama little black boys and black girls will join hands with little white boys and white girls as sisters and brothers. I have a dream today"*

Sports, for all of their undeniable athletic and active feats, would suffer in the absence of words. Just imagine a stadium devoid of its crowds, a television game without commentary, or even a park on a Sunday morning lacking the chorus of the sideline. Sport is one of many arenas in life where words and action marry for better effect. There is an endless list of great sporting moments which have been defined and greatly influenced by words in the form of commentary.

I must disclaim, that not for a moment am I trying to take anything away from those who have created such moments of history with their actions. I am simply trying to prove and make clear the existence of the logocracy as a defining factor in history. Actions are a supreme force of nature, and a leader of society in their own right, however, words ought not be underestimated, nor is their rule over the past, the present, and the future in the form of a logocracy.

We are defined by words

We, as humans, are the greatest source of proof that the Logocracy exists. There is no doubt that we are governed by the Logocracy. We do choose, however, how we are governed, moreover, how to govern with it. An excellent article by the BRM institute titled 'The Neuroscience behind our words' explains this fact very well. Maria Richter and several other scientists conducted an experiment on 16 different people titled 'Do words hurt?' According to the BRM institute, the scientists discovered 'painful or negative words increase implicit processing (IMP) within the subgenual anterior cingulate cortex' In simple terms, their experiment proved that

"negative words release stress and anxiety inducing hormones in subjects"

However, there are two sides to every story. Words can also have a positive effect upon our brains, hence upon our lives. The BRM Institute cites the book 'Words can change your brain' by Dr. Andrew Newberg and Mark Robert Waldman. The authors state that:

"By holding a positive and optimistic (word) in your mind, you stimulate frontal lobe activity. This area includes specific language centres that connect directly to the motor cortex responsible for moving you into action. And as our research has shown, the longer you concentrate on positive words, the more you begin to affect other areas of the brain'"

Waldman and Newberg also emphasize the importance of one single word:

> *"A single word has the power to influence the expression of genes that regulate physical and emotional stress"*

Based on the aforementioned research, it is clear that we are governed by a Logocracy. However, it is equally clear that this form of governance involves no dictator, rather, we all partake and contribute, but most importantly, we all own the choice of how exactly we are governed by the Logocracy, better yet, how to govern with it.

How to use guide

The 'Logocracy' word journal is intended for daily use in the 2022 calendar year. Each day has been assigned a different word to engage with. There is a wide and interesting variety of words, some that might not seem relative to you however such is a choice of perception. You can choose to make this word relevant to you by thinking about it, by spending time with it, these are the first and most important steps. Each day has two separate sections, one for the morning and one for the evening. In both of these sections you will be asked to answer the question of 'What does this word mean to you?' This is where the diversity and intrigue of the journal lies as each and every user will have a different answer for the same word, their own answer.

Beneath the morning and evening sections there is a space to rewrite the meaning of the word followed by a space to write a sentence including the word. Once you begin to use this word journal, you will realise just how this daily interaction with words relates directly to the Logocracy in a positive way.

The use of this word journal involves three integral aspects of our development:

1) Thought
2) Opening the mind
3) Learning

Taking just a few minutes out of each day we manage to think about this new word, to open our minds to this new word, and to learn this new word. You need to allow your mind to wander, to be curious, to make something of each word, to create, to develop, to interact, to shape, to ponder, to discover, to ask questions. Despite this section of the introduction being a 'how to use guide', I cannot tell you how to think. Such is the beauty of the Logocracy. It is yours. You can choose how to think, to allow your mind to be opened and improved by one single word each day.

SATURDAY JANUARY 1ST

Ameliorate ~ To improve/make something better
AH - ME - LEE - YUR - ATE

{Morning} What does this word mean to you?

{Evening} What does this word mean to you?

Meaning:

Sentence:

Sunday January 2nd

Multifarious ~ having great diversity
MUL - TEE - FAIR - EE - US

{Morning} What does this word mean to you?

{Evening} What does this word mean to you?

Meaning:

Sentence:

Monday January 3rd

Deipnosophy ~ debate or conversation at the dinner table

DEE - EP - NOH - SO - PHEE

{Morning} What does this word mean to you?

{Evening} What does this word mean to you?

Meaning:

Sentence:

Tuesday January 4th

Kainotophobia ~ a fear of change
KANE - OH - TO - PHO - BIA

{Morning} What does this word mean to you?

{Evening} What does this word mean to you?

Meaning:

Sentence:

Wednesday January 5th

Quaestuary ~ concerned with profit; money making
QEE - STEW - REE

{*Morning*} *What does this word mean to you?*

{*Evening*} *What does this word mean to you?*

Meaning:

Sentence:

Gainsay ~ To speak against or oppose
GAIN - SAY

{Morning} What does this word mean to you?

{Evening} What does this word mean to you?

Meaning:

Sentence:

Vacillate ~ To waver between different actions; Indecisive
VASS - ILL - ATE

{*Morning*} *What does this word mean to you?*

{*Evening*} *What does this word mean to you?*

Meaning:

Sentence:

SATURDAY JANUARY 8TH

Bathmism ~ a hypothetical growth force
BATH - MISM

{Morning} What does this word mean to you?

{Evening} What does this word mean to you?

Meaning:

Sentence:

Sunday January 9th

Xenagogue ~ Someone who guides strangers or new arrivals
ZEE - NA - GOG

{*Morning*} *What does this word mean to you?*

{*Evening*} *What does this word mean to you?*

Meaning:

Sentence:

MONDAY JANUARY 10TH

Jannock ~ straightforward and fair; upright, honest
JANN - OCK

{*Morning*} *What does this word mean to you?*

{*Evening*} *What does this word mean to you?*

Meaning:

Sentence:

Tuesday January 11th

Paideutics ~ the science or art of teaching
PEE - DEE - YOU - TICKS

{Morning} What does this word mean to you?

{Evening} What does this word mean to you?

Meaning:

Sentence:

WEDNESDAY JANUARY 12TH

Canophilia ~ A love of dogs
CANE - O - PHEE - LEE - AH

{Morning} What does this word mean to you?

{Evening} What does this word mean to you?

Meaning:

Sentence:

Obambulate ~ To walk about or wander
OH - BAMB - YOU - LATE

{Morning} What does this word mean to you?

{Evening} What does this word mean to you?

Meaning:

Sentence:

Raissoneur ~ central character who voices theme
REZ - UH - NUR

{Morning} *What does this word mean to you?*

{Evening} *What does this word mean to you?*

Meaning:

Sentence:

SATURDAY JANUARY 15TH

Ecdemomania ~ a compulsion to travel or go outside
ECK - DEM - OH - MANIA

{*Morning*} *What does this word mean to you?*

{*Evening*} *What does this word mean to you?*

Meaning:

Sentence:

SUNDAY JANUARY 16TH

Nadir ~ *the lowest point*
NAH - DEAR

{Morning} What does this word mean to you?

{Evening} What does this word mean to you?

Meaning:

Sentence:

Monday January 17th

Ideopraxist ~ a person who embodies an idea in an action
ID - EE - OH - PRAX - IST

{Morning} What does this word mean to you?

{Evening} What does this word mean to you?

Meaning:

Sentence:

TUESDAY JANUARY 18TH

Salubrious ~ *health giving; healthy;pleasant*

SAL - OO - BREE - US

{*Morning*} *What does this word mean to you?*

{*Evening*} *What does this word mean to you?*

Meaning:

Sentence:

WEDNESDAY JANUARY 19TH

Facundity ~ effective in communication; eloquent speech
FA - CUN - DIH - TEE

{*Morning*} *What does this word mean to you?*

{*Evening*} *What does this word mean to you?*

Meaning:

Sentence:

Thursday January 20th

Lachrymose ~ causing tears; sad; given to tears/weeping
LACK - REE - MOSE

{Morning} What does this word mean to you?

{Evening} What does this word mean to you?

Meaning:

Sentence:

FRIDAY JANUARY 21ST

Haecceity ~ the property of being a unique, individual thing
HECK - SEE - ET - EE

{Morning} What does this word mean to you?

{Evening} What does this word mean to you?

Meaning:

Sentence:

Zephyr ~ *a soft gentle breeze*
ZEF - ER

{*Morning*} *What does this word mean to you?*

{*Evening*} *What does this word mean to you?*

Meaning:

Sentence:

SUNDAY JANUARY 23RD

Deleterious ~ causing harm or damage
DEL - EH - TEAR - EE - US

{*Morning*} *What does this word mean to you?*

{*Evening*} *What does this word mean to you?*

Meaning:

Sentence:

Waygone ~ wearied by travel
WAY - GONE

{*Morning*} *What does this word mean to you?*

_____

_____

_____

_____

_____

_____

{*Evening*} *What does this word mean to you?*

_____

_____

_____

_____

_____

Meaning:

_____

Sentence:

_____

_____

TUESDAY JANUARY 25TH

Zelotypia ~ excessively jealous or obsessive
ZEL - OH - TIP - EE - AH

{*Morning*} *What does this word mean to you?*

{*Evening*} *What does this word mean to you?*

Meaning:

Sentence:

WEDNESDAY JANUARY 26TH

Negaholic ~ one with a persistently pessimistic outlook or attitude

NEG - AH - HOL - ICK

{Morning} What does this word mean to you?

{Evening} What does this word mean to you?

Meaning:

Sentence:

Petrichor ~ *the smell after rain following a dry period of weather*

PEH - TRI - CORE

{*Morning*} *What does this word mean to you?*

{*Evening*} *What does this word mean to you?*

Meaning:

Sentence:

Friday January 28th

Macrobian ~ *long living; having a long life span*
MAH - CROW - BEE - IN

{*Morning*} *What does this word mean to you?*

{*Evening*} *What does this word mean to you?*

Meaning:

Sentence:

SATURDAY JANUARY 29TH

Ubiquarian ~ one who is everywhere at once
YOU - BICK - WEAR - EE - AN

{*Morning*} *What does this word mean to you?*

{*Evening*} *What does this word mean to you?*

Meaning:

Sentence:

Sunday January 30th

Tacenda ~ things better left unsaid

TA - SEND - AH

{Morning} What does this word mean to you?

{Evening} What does this word mean to you?

Meaning:

Sentence:

MONDAY JANUARY 31ST

Vaniloquence ~ vain or foolish talk
VAN - ILL - OH - QUENCE

{*Morning*} *What does this word mean to you?*

{*Evening*} *What does this word mean to you?*

Meaning:

Sentence:

Vernal ~ *of, relating to, or happening in the Spring*
VER - NULL

{Morning} What does this word mean to you?

{Evening} What does this word mean to you?

Meaning:

Sentence:

Wednesday February 2nd

Captious ~ tending to find fault; critical
CAP - SHUS

{*Morning*} *What does this word mean to you?*

{*Evening*} *What does this word mean to you?*

Meaning:

Sentence:

Thursday February 3rd

Oblectation ~ a state of being greatly pleased; delight;
enjoyment
OB - LECK - TAY - SHUN

{*Morning*} *What does this word mean to you?*

{*Evening*} *What does this word mean to you?*

Meaning:

Sentence:

FRIDAY FEBRUARY 4TH

Edacious ~ having an insatiable appetite; greedy
EE - DAY - SHUS

{Morning} What does this word mean to you?

{Evening} What does this word mean to you?

Meaning:

Sentence:

Saturday February 5th

Sangfroid ~ composure or coolness in tough circumstances
SANG - FREUD

{Morning} What does this word mean to you?

{Evening} What does this word mean to you?

Meaning:

Sentence:

SUNDAY FEBRUARY 6TH

Taphephobia ~ fear of being buried alive
TAFF - EH - PHOBIA

{Morning} What does this word mean to you?

{Evening} What does this word mean to you?

Meaning:

Sentence:

Xenodocheionology ~ the love; study; history of hotels
ZENO - DOH - KEY - OH - NOLOGY

{*Morning*} *What does this word mean to you?*

{*Evening*} *What does this word mean to you?*

Meaning:

Sentence:

TUESDAY FEBRUARY 8TH

Pandiculation ~ the act of yawning whilst stretching
PAN - DICK - YOU - LAY - SHUN

{*Morning*} *What does this word mean to you?*

{*Evening*} *What does this word mean to you?*

Meaning:

Sentence:

Laetificate ~ *to make or become happy; to enrich*
LAY - TIF - IH - KIT

{*Morning*} *What does this word mean to you?*

{*Evening*} *What does this word mean to you?*

Meaning:

Sentence:

Thursday February 10th

Ignoscency ~ forgiveness; forgiving spirit
IG - NAWH - SEN - SEE

{Morning} What does this word mean to you?

_____

_____

_____

_____

_____

_____

{Evening} What does this word mean to you?

_____

_____

_____

_____

_____

_____

Meaning:

_____

Sentence:

_____

_____

Friday February 11th

Magniloquent ~ using high flown or bombastic language
MAG - NIL - OH - QUENT

{*Morning*} *What does this word mean to you?*

{*Evening*} *What does this word mean to you?*

Meaning:

Sentence:

SATURDAY FEBRUARY 12TH

Dendrophilous ~ *tree loving; living on or thriving in trees*
DEN - DRO - FILE - US

{*Morning*} *What does this word mean to you?*

{*Evening*} *What does this word mean to you?*

Meaning:

Sentence:

SUNDAY FEBRUARY 13TH

Fastigium ~ the apex or summit of something
FAS - STIJ - EE - UM

{*Morning*} *What does this word mean to you?*

{*Evening*} *What does this word mean to you?*

Meaning:

Sentence:

Monday February 14th

Ataraxia ~ a state of serene calmness
AT - AH - RAX - EE - AH

{*Morning*} *What does this word mean to you?*

{*Evening*} *What does this word mean to you?*

Meaning:

Sentence:

Hamartia ~ a character flaw which leads to downfall

HAM - ARE - SHE - AH

{Morning} *What does this word mean to you?*

{Evening} *What does this word mean to you?*

Meaning:

Sentence:

WEDNESDAY FEBRUARY 16TH

Gastrophilanthropist ~ one who seeks to satisfy others'
appetites
GASTRO - PHIL - AN - THROW - PIST

{Morning} What does this word mean to you?

{Evening} What does this word mean to you?

Meaning:

Sentence:

Thursday February 17th

Negotiosity ~ the state of being busy; engaged in business
NEG - OH - TEE - OSS - IT - EE

{Morning} What does this word mean to you?

{Evening} What does this word mean to you?

Meaning:

Sentence:

Velleity ~ *a wish or feeling not strong enough to lead to action*
VELL - EE - EH - TEE

{*Morning*} *What does this word mean to you?*

{*Evening*} *What does this word mean to you?*

Meaning:

Sentence:

Saturday February 19th

Quaestuary ~ concerned with profit; money making
KWEE - STEW - REE

{*Morning*} *What does this word mean to you?*

{*Evening*} *What does this word mean to you?*

Meaning:

Sentence:

Sunday February 20th

Ughten ~ early morning; period of twilight before dawn
YOU - TUN

{*Morning*} *What does this word mean to you?*

{*Evening*} *What does this word mean to you?*

Meaning:

Sentence:

Monday February 21st

Tarriance ~ *the act of delaying; procrastinating*

TARR - EE - ANCE

{*Morning*} *What does this word mean to you?*

{*Evening*} *What does this word mean to you?*

Meaning:

Sentence:

Bellwether ~ leading sheep in flock; someone who leads
BELL - WEATHER

{*Morning*} *What does this word mean to you?*

{*Evening*} *What does this word mean to you?*

Meaning:

Sentence:

Oblivescence ~ the process of forgetting
OB - LIVE - ESS - INCE

{Morning} What does this word mean to you?

_____

_____

_____

_____

_____

_____

_____

{Evening} What does this word mean to you?

_____

_____

_____

_____

_____

_____

_____

Meaning:

_____

Sentence:

_____

_____

Catarolysis ~ letting off steam by cursing
CAT - AH - ROL - IH - SIS

{*Morning*} *What does this word mean to you?*

{*Evening*} *What does this word mean to you?*

Meaning:

Sentence:

Friday February 25th

Egestuous ~ desperately poor
EE - JEST - YOU - US

{Morning} What does this word mean to you?

{Evening} What does this word mean to you?

Meaning:

Sentence:

SATURDAY FEBRUARY 26TH

Panmnesia ~ remembrance of everything; flawless memory
PAN - MNE - SHE - AH

{Morning} What does this word mean to you?

{Evening} What does this word mean to you?

Meaning:

Sentence:

Sunday February 27th

Mammonism ~ the greedy pursuit of riches
MAM - ON - ISM

{Morning} What does this word mean to you?

{Evening} What does this word mean to you?

Meaning:

Sentence:

Monday February 28th

Selcouth ~ odd or extraordinary; peculiar
SELL - COO - TH

{*Morning*} *What does this word mean to you?*

{*Evening*} *What does this word mean to you?*

Meaning:

Sentence:

TUESDAY MARCH 1ST

Vasculature ~ network of blood vessels joining heart to organs

VASS - QUE - LAY - TURE

{Morning} What does this word mean to you?

{Evening} What does this word mean to you?

Meaning:

Sentence:

WEDNESDAY MARCH 2ND

Lepid ~ pleasant; amusing
LEH - PID

{Morning} What does this word mean to you?

{Evening} What does this word mean to you?

Meaning:

Sentence:

THURSDAY MARCH 3RD

Sempiternal ~ eternal; unchanging; everlasting
SEMP - IH - TER - NAL

{Morning} What does this word mean to you?

{Evening} What does this word mean to you?

Meaning:

Sentence:

FRIDAY MARCH 4TH

Ultracrepidarian ~ someone who gives opinions on things they have little knowledge of UL - TRA - KREP - I - DARE - IEN

{Morning} What does this word mean to you?

{Evening} What does this word mean to you?

Meaning:

Sentence:

---

illecebrous ~ *tending to attract; enticing*
IL - LE - CE - BRO - US

{*Morning*} *What does this word mean to you?*

{*Evening*} *What does this word mean to you?*

Meaning:

Sentence:

Sunday March 6th

Redolent ~ reminiscent of; sweet smelling
RED - UH - LENT

{Morning} What does this word mean to you?

{Evening} What does this word mean to you?

Meaning:

Sentence:

Nemophilist ~ one who is fond of or loves forests
NEM - OH - PHIL - IST

{Morning} What does this word mean to you?

{Evening} What does this word mean to you?

Meaning:

Sentence:

TUESDAY MARCH 8TH

Autognosis ~ self knowledge; an understanding of oneself
AU - TOG - NO - SIS

{Morning} What does this word mean to you?

{Evening} What does this word mean to you?

Meaning:

Sentence:

WEDNESDAY MARCH 9TH

Felicificative ~ tending to make happy
FE - LI - CI - FIC - AT - IVE

{*Morning*} *What does this word mean to you?*

{*Evening*} *What does this word mean to you?*

Meaning:

Sentence:

Thursday March 10th

Gaudiloquent ~ *speaking with joy or happiness*
GAW - DIL - OH - QUENT

{*Morning*} *What does this word mean to you?*

{*Evening*} *What does this word mean to you?*

Meaning:

Sentence:

Hebdomadal ~ *occurring weekly*
HEB - DOM - A - DUL

{*Morning*} *What does this word mean to you?*

{*Evening*} *What does this word mean to you?*

Meaning:

Sentence:

Saturday March 12th

Deoppilate ~ to free from obstruction
DEE - OP - ILL - ATE

{Morning} What does this word mean to you?

{Evening} What does this word mean to you?

Meaning:

Sentence:

Pantoglot ~ one who understands or uses all languages
PAN - TOE - GLOT

{*Morning*} *What does this word mean to you?*

{*Evening*} *What does this word mean to you?*

Meaning:

Sentence:

Typhlophile ~ a person who devotes themself to helping the blind
TIFF - LOW - PHILE

{*Morning*} *What does this word mean to you?*

{*Evening*} *What does this word mean to you?*

Meaning:

Sentence:

Marigenous ~ produced in or by the sea

MAR - IG - EE - NUS

{Morning} What does this word mean to you?

{Evening} What does this word mean to you?

Meaning:

Sentence:

Eleemosynary ~ charitable; related to or depending on charity
EL - EE - MO - SIGN - AIR - EE

{Morning} What does this word mean to you?

{Evening} What does this word mean to you?

Meaning:

Sentence:

Smaragdine ~ of, or like an emerald green; related to emeralds

SMAR - AG - DINE

{Morning} What does this word mean to you?

{Evening} What does this word mean to you?

Meaning:

Sentence:

Friday March 18th

Cathexis ~ allocation of mental or emotional energy to something
CA - THEX - IS

{Morning} What does this word mean to you?

_____

_____

_____

_____

_____

{Evening} What does this word mean to you?

_____

_____

_____

_____

_____

Meaning:

_____

_____

Sentence:

_____

_____

Saturday March 19th

Kakorrhaphiophobia ~ the fear of failure
KAK - ORR - HA - PHIO - PHOBIA

{*Morning*} *What does this word mean to you?*

{*Evening*} *What does this word mean to you?*

Meaning:

Sentence:

Ventripotent ~ having a large appetite; gluttonous
VEN - TREE - PO - TENT

{Morning} What does this word mean to you?

{Evening} What does this word mean to you?

Meaning:

Sentence:

Welkin ~ the sky or heavens
WEL - KIN

{*Morning*} *What does this word mean to you?*

{*Evening*} *What does this word mean to you?*

Meaning:

Sentence:

TUESDAY MARCH 22ND

Teleonomy ~ *the condition of having a purpose*
TEL - EE - ON - OM - EE

{*Morning*} *What does this word mean to you?*

{*Evening*} *What does this word mean to you?*

Meaning:

Sentence:

Latitudinarian ~ *not insisting on conformity to one doctrine; open*

LAT - IH - TUDE - IN - AIR - EE - AN

{Morning} What does this word mean to you?

{Evening} What does this word mean to you?

Meaning:

Sentence:

THURSDAY MARCH 24TH

Jentacular ~ *of or pertaining to breakfast*

JENT - ACK - YOU - LAR

{*Morning*} *What does this word mean to you?*

{*Evening*} *What does this word mean to you?*

Meaning:

Sentence:

Friday March 25th

Adamantine ~ unable to broken
AD - AM - AN - TINE

{Morning} What does this word mean to you?

{Evening} What does this word mean to you?

Meaning:

Sentence:

Saturday March 26th

Neophobe ~ fear of anything new or of innovation
NEO - PHOBE

{Morning} What does this word mean to you?

{Evening} What does this word mean to you?

Meaning:

Sentence:

SUNDAY MARCH 27TH

Yapness ~ hunger
YAP - NESS

{Morning} What does this word mean to you?

{Evening} What does this word mean to you?

Meaning:

Sentence:

93

MONDAY MARCH 28TH

Panurgic ~ able or ready to do anything
PAN - ER - JICK

{Morning} What does this word mean to you?

{Evening} What does this word mean to you?

Meaning:

Sentence:

Sesquipedalian ~ *of a word {long}; tending to use long words*
SES - QUIP - EH - DAY - LEE - AN

{Morning} What does this word mean to you?

{Evening} What does this word mean to you?

Meaning:

Sentence:

WEDNESDAY MARCH 30TH

Aeviternity ~ eternity; everlasting existence
AY - VIT - ER - NIT - EE

{*Morning*} *What does this word mean to you?*

{*Evening*} *What does this word mean to you?*

Meaning:

Sentence:

illimitable ~ *without limits or an end*

iLL - IM - IT - ABLE

{*Morning*} *What does this word mean to you?*

{*Evening*} *What does this word mean to you?*

Meaning:

Sentence:

Friday April 1st

Didascalic ~ intended to teach; relating to teaching
DIE - DAH - SCAL - ICK

{*Morning*} *What does this word mean to you?*

{*Evening*} *What does this word mean to you?*

Meaning:

Sentence:

Feracious ~ producing abundantly; prolific
FUR - AY - SHUS

{Morning} What does this word mean to you?

{Evening} What does this word mean to you?

Meaning:

Sentence:

Sunday April 3rd

Matripotestal ~ of or relating to the power of mothers
MAH - TREE - POH - TEST - UL

{*Morning*} *What does this word mean to you?*

{*Evening*} *What does this word mean to you?*

Meaning:

Sentence:

MONDAY APRIL 4TH

Henotic ~ promoting peace; serving to reconcile
HEN - OT - ICK

{*Morning*} *What does this word mean to you?*

{*Evening*} *What does this word mean to you?*

Meaning:

Sentence:

TUESDAY APRIL 5TH

Logophile ~ a lover of words
LOG - O - PHILE

{Morning} What does this word mean to you?

{Evening} What does this word mean to you?

Meaning:

Sentence:

WEDNESDAY APRIL 6TH

Querimonious ~ prone to complaining; full of complaint
QWE - RIH - MOAN - EE - YUS

{*Morning*} *What does this word mean to you?*

{*Evening*} *What does this word mean to you?*

Meaning:

Sentence:

THURSDAY APRIL 7TH

Ochlophobia ~ extreme fear or dislike of crowds
OCK - LOW - FOE - BEE - AH

{Morning} *What does this word mean to you?*

{Evening} *What does this word mean to you?*

Meaning:

Sentence:

FRIDAY APRIL 8TH

Sipid ~ having a pleasant taste or flavor
SIH - PID

{*Morning*} *What does this word mean to you?*

{*Evening*} *What does this word mean to you?*

Meaning:

Sentence:

SATURDAY APRIL 9TH

Catholicon ~ a solution for all difficulties; remedy for all diseases
CAH - THOL - IH - CON

{*Morning*} *What does this word mean to you?*

{*Evening*} *What does this word mean to you?*

Meaning:

Sentence:

Bibliognost ~ a book lover; one with great knowledge of books
BIB - LEE - OH - NOST

{Morning} What does this word mean to you?

{Evening} What does this word mean to you?

Meaning:

Sentence:

Monday April 11th

Telesis ~ progress that is intelligently planned and directed; deliberate use of nature to obtain goals TELL - EE - SIS

{*Morning*} *What does this word mean to you?*

{*Evening*} *What does this word mean to you?*

Meaning:

Sentence:

TUESDAY APRIL 12TH

Parciloquy ~ the quality of speaking little; laconic
PAR - SILL - OH - QWEE

{*Morning*} *What does this word mean to you?*

{*Evening*} *What does this word mean to you?*

Meaning:

Sentence:

WEDNESDAY APRIL 13TH

Legerity ~ *quickness of mind and body*
LEH - JAIR - IH - TEE

{*Morning*} *What does this word mean to you?*

{*Evening*} *What does this word mean to you?*

Meaning:

Sentence:

THURSDAY APRIL 14TH

Nephalism ~ total abstinence from alcohol
NEFF - AL - ISM

{Morning} What does this word mean to you?

{Evening} What does this word mean to you?

Meaning:

Sentence:

FRIDAY APRIL 15TH

Ultroneous ~ spontaneous; voluntary
ULL - TRO - NEE - US

{Morning} What does this word mean to you?

{Evening} What does this word mean to you?

Meaning:

Sentence:

SATURDAY APRIL 16TH

Sisyphean ~ something {a task} that cannot be completed
SIS - EE - FEE - AN

{*Morning*} *What does this word mean to you?*

{*Evening*} *What does this word mean to you?*

Meaning:

Sentence:

SUNDAY APRIL 17TH

Veracious ~ speaking or representing the truth
VUR - AY - SHUS

{Morning} What does this word mean to you?

{Evening} What does this word mean to you?

Meaning:

Sentence:

MONDAY APRIL 18TH

Xenodochial ~ friendly to strangers
ZEE - NO - DOH - KEY - AL

{*Morning*} *What does this word mean to you?*

{*Evening*} *What does this word mean to you?*

Meaning:

Sentence:

TUESDAY APRIL 19TH

Matutinal ~ of, or relating to, or occurring in the morning
MAT - YOU - TIN - AL

{Morning} What does this word mean to you?

{Evening} What does this word mean to you?

Meaning:

Sentence:

Agathokakological ~ *consisting of both good and evil*
AG - ATH - OH - KAK - OH - LOGIC - AL

{*Morning*} *What does this word mean to you?*

{*Evening*} *What does this word mean to you?*

Meaning:

Sentence:

Thursday April 21st

Dippydro ~ a person who often changes their mind
DIP - EE - DRO

{*Morning*} *What does this word mean to you?*

{*Evening*} *What does this word mean to you?*

Meaning:

Sentence:

Friday April 22nd

Redintegrate ~ restore something to a state of perfection or unity

RED - IN - TEG - RATE

{Morning} *What does this word mean to you?*

{Evening} *What does this word mean to you?*

Meaning:

Sentence:

SATURDAY APRIL 23RD

Temporicide ~ killing time
TEMP - OR - IH - CIDE

{*Morning*} *What does this word mean to you?*

{*Evening*} *What does this word mean to you?*

Meaning:

Sentence:

Imbroglio ~ an extremely complicated or embarrassing situation

IM - BRO - LEE - OH

{*Morning*} *What does this word mean to you?*

{*Evening*} *What does this word mean to you?*

Meaning:

Sentence:

MONDAY APRIL 25TH

Encraty ~ the control of one's desires and actions
EN - CRAT - EE

{Morning} What does this word mean to you?

{Evening} What does this word mean to you?

Meaning:

Sentence:

Flexiloquent ~ speaking doubtfully or doubly
FLEX - ILL - OH - QUENT

{*Morning*} *What does this word mean to you?*

{*Evening*} *What does this word mean to you?*

Meaning:

Sentence:

WEDNESDAY APRIL 27TH

Obtenebrate ~ to darken; to cast a shadow over
OB - TEN - EH - BRATE

{Morning} What does this word mean to you?

{Evening} What does this word mean to you?

Meaning:

Sentence:

THURSDAY APRIL 28TH

Gelid ~ extremely cold; icy
GEL - ID

{Morning} What does this word mean to you?

_____

_____

_____

_____

_____

_____

_____

{Evening} What does this word mean to you?

_____

_____

_____

_____

_____

_____

Meaning:

_____

Sentence:

_____

_____

FRIDAY APRIL 29TH

Hesternopothia ~ yearning for the past
HESS - TER - NO - POE - THEE - AH

{*Morning*} *What does this word mean to you?*

{*Evening*} *What does this word mean to you?*

Meaning:

Sentence:

Parvanimity ~ small minded; mean
PAR - VA - NIM - IH - TEE

{*Morning*} *What does this word mean to you?*

{*Evening*} *What does this word mean to you?*

Meaning:

Sentence:

SUNDAY MAY 1ST

Chrematistic ~ of, or relating to money making
CREM - AH - TIST - ICK

{*Morning*} *What does this word mean to you?*

{*Evening*} *What does this word mean to you?*

Meaning:

Sentence:

Monday May 2nd

Nephelococcygia ~ *the act of finding shapes in clouds*

NEF - EL - OH - COCK - CIG - EE - AH

{*Morning*} *What does this word mean to you?*

_____

_____

_____

_____

_____

_____

_____

{*Evening*} *What does this word mean to you?*

_____

_____

_____

_____

_____

_____

_____

Meaning:

_____

_____

Sentence:

_____

_____

TUESDAY MAY 3RD

Wiseacre ~ a person with an affection for knowledge
WISE - ACHE - ER

{Morning} What does this word mean to you?

{Evening} What does this word mean to you?

Meaning:

Sentence:

Lenity ~ the quality of being kind and gentle
LEN - IT - EE

{Morning} *What does this word mean to you?*

{Evening} *What does this word mean to you?*

Meaning:

Sentence:

THURSDAY MAY 5TH

Matutolypea ~ *waking up on the wrong side of the bed*
MA - TU - TOE - LIE - PEE - AH

{*Morning*} *What does this word mean to you?*

{*Evening*} *What does this word mean to you?*

Meaning:

Sentence:

Friday May 6th

Spatiotemporal ~ belonging to, or relating to both space and time

SPAY - SHEE - OH - TEMP - OR - AL

{*Morning*} *What does this word mean to you?*

{*Evening*} *What does this word mean to you?*

Meaning:

Sentence:

Saturday May 7th

Temulence ~ drunkenness; intoxication
TEM - U - LENCE

{*Morning*} *What does this word mean to you?*

{*Evening*} *What does this word mean to you?*

Meaning:

Sentence:

SUNDAY MAY 8TH

Verbomania ~ *obsession with or love of words*
VERB - O - MANIA

{*Morning*} *What does this word mean to you?*

{*Evening*} *What does this word mean to you?*

Meaning:

Sentence:

Monday May 9th

Pedagogue ~ *a teacher*
PEE - DA - GOG

{Morning} *What does this word mean to you?*

{Evening} *What does this word mean to you?*

Meaning:

Sentence:

TUESDAY MAY 10TH

Undulating ~ moving up and down in waves {a landscape}
UN - DUE - LAY - TING

{*Morning*} *What does this word mean to you?*

{*Evening*} *What does this word mean to you?*

Meaning:

Sentence:

WEDNESDAY MAY 11TH

Dipsomania ~ an uncontrollable craving for alcohol
DIP - SO - MAY - NEE - AH

{Morning} What does this word mean to you?

{Evening} What does this word mean to you?

Meaning:

Sentence:

Thursday May 12th

Apolaustic ~ dedicated to enjoyment
AP - OH - LAO - STICK

{Morning} *What does this word mean to you?*

{Evening} *What does this word mean to you?*

Meaning:

Sentence:

Vicambulate ~ to walk about in the streets
VI - CAM - BU - LATE

{*Morning*} *What does this word mean to you?*

{*Evening*} *What does this word mean to you?*

Meaning:

Sentence:

Zoism ~ reverence for animal life; belief in animal power
ZO - ISM

{*Morning*} *What does this word mean to you?*

{*Evening*} *What does this word mean to you?*

Meaning:

Sentence:

SUNDAY MAY 15TH

Entelechy ~ the realization of potential
EN - TEL - ECK - EE

{*Morning*} *What does this word mean to you?*

{*Evening*} *What does this word mean to you?*

Meaning:

Sentence:

Monday May 16th

Gelogenic ~ inducing or provoking laughter
GEL - O - GEN - ICK

{*Morning*} *What does this word mean to you?*

{*Evening*} *What does this word mean to you?*

Meaning:

Sentence:

Tuesday May 17th

Oikology ~ *the science of housekeeping; the cleanliness of a home* OI - KOL - OGY

{Morning} What does this word mean to you?

{Evening} What does this word mean to you?

Meaning:

Sentence:

WEDNESDAY MAY 18TH

Impavid ~ fearless; undaunted
IM - PAV - ID

{Morning} What does this word mean to you?

{Evening} What does this word mean to you?

Meaning:

Sentence:

Thursday May 19th

Quiddity ~ whatever makes something what it is; essence
QUID - IT - TEE

{Morning} What does this word mean to you?

{Evening} What does this word mean to you?

Meaning:

Sentence:

Halcyon ~ calm; peaceful; tranquil; a happy time in the past
HAL - SEE - YON

{Morning} What does this word mean to you?

{Evening} What does this word mean to you?

Meaning:

Sentence:

SATURDAY MAY 21ST

Mellisonant ~ sweet sounding; peaceful to the ear
MEL - EE - SON - ANT

{*Morning*} *What does this word mean to you?*

{*Evening*} *What does this word mean to you?*

Meaning:

Sentence:

Penury ~ the state of being very poor; extreme poverty
PEN - YUR - EE

{*Morning*} *What does this word mean to you?*

{*Evening*} *What does this word mean to you?*

Meaning:

Sentence:

Monday May 23rd

Chronosynchronicity ~ presentation of all stages of a person's life in one piece of art
CHRONO - SINK - RON - I - CITY

{*Morning*} *What does this word mean to you?*

{*Evening*} *What does this word mean to you?*

Meaning:

Sentence:

TUESDAY MAY 24TH

Heuristic ~ enabling someone to learn something themselves
HEW - RIS - TIC

{Morning} What does this word mean to you?

{Evening} What does this word mean to you?

Meaning:

Sentence:

WEDNESDAY MAY 25TH

Blandiloquent ~ mild, flattering speech
BLAN - DIL - O - QUENT

{Morning} What does this word mean to you?

{Evening} What does this word mean to you?

Meaning:

Sentence:

Libricide ~ the destruction of books
LIB - RI - CIDE

{Morning} What does this word mean to you?

{Evening} What does this word mean to you?

Meaning:

Sentence:

Friday May 27th

Solivagant ~ *wandering alone*
SOL - EE - VAY - JANT

{Morning} *What does this word mean to you?*

{Evening} *What does this word mean to you?*

Meaning:

Sentence:

Tergiversate ~ *to change one's loyalties continually*
TER - GIVE - ER - SATE

{Morning} What does this word mean to you?

{Evening} What does this word mean to you?

Meaning:

Sentence:

Natalitial ~ of, or relating to birthdays
NAY - TAL - I - TIAL

{Morning} What does this word mean to you?

{Evening} What does this word mean to you?

Meaning:

Sentence:

Kalon ~ physical and moral beauty
KAY - LON

{*Morning*} *What does this word mean to you?*

{*Evening*} *What does this word mean to you?*

Meaning:

Sentence:

Tuesday May 31st

Diuturnal ~ long lasting; continual
DIE - YOU - TURN - AL

{*Morning*} *What does this word mean to you?*

{*Evening*} *What does this word mean to you?*

Meaning:

Sentence:

Vesuviate ~ to burst forth like an eruption
VES - OO - VEE - ATE

{Morning} What does this word mean to you?

{Evening} What does this word mean to you?

Meaning:

Sentence:

THURSDAY JUNE 2ND

Somniloquence ~ the act of talking in ones sleep
SOM - NIL - O - QUENCE

{*Morning*} *What does this word mean to you?*

{*Evening*} *What does this word mean to you?*

Meaning:

Sentence:

FRIDAY JUNE 3RD

Agersia ~ the quality of not growing old
AG - ER - SIA

{Morning} What does this word mean to you?

{Evening} What does this word mean to you?

Meaning:

Sentence:

SATURDAY JUNE 4TH

Eosophobia ~ a fear of the dawn or daylight
EO - SO - PHO - BIA

{Morning} What does this word mean to you?

{Evening} What does this word mean to you?

Meaning:

Sentence:

Sunday June 5th

Jobation ~ an extensive rebuke or reprimand; persecution
JO - BAY - SHUN

{Morning} What does this word mean to you?

{Evening} What does this word mean to you?

Meaning:

Sentence:

Meliorism ~ the belief that the world can be made better by Human effort ME - LEE - OH - RISM

{Morning} What does this word mean to you?

{Evening} What does this word mean to you?

Meaning:

Sentence:

Tuesday June 7th

Oikonisus ~ desire to start a family
OI - KON - I - SUS

{Morning} What does this word mean to you?

{Evening} What does this word mean to you?

Meaning:

Sentence:

WEDNESDAY JUNE 8TH

Rencounter ~ *a chance meeting with someone*
REN - COUNT - ER

{Morning} What does this word mean to you?

{Evening} What does this word mean to you?

Meaning:

Sentence:

Thursday June 9th

Geoselenic ~ *of or relating to the moon and earth; their mutual relation or connection*

GEO - SEL - EN - IC

{Morning} What does this word mean to you?

{Evening} What does this word mean to you?

Meaning:

Sentence:

FRIDAY JUNE 10TH

Thalassophile ~ a lover of the sea
THAL - ASS - O - PHILE

{*Morning*} *What does this word mean to you?*

{*Evening*} *What does this word mean to you?*

Meaning:

Sentence:

Saturday June 11th

Imperseverant ~ lacking the power to perceive; thoughtless
IM - PER - SEV - ER - ANT

{Morning} What does this word mean to you?

{Evening} What does this word mean to you?

Meaning:

Sentence:

SUNDAY JUNE 12TH

Peripeteia ~ a sudden change in fortune or circumstance
PERI - PET - EYE - AH

{*Morning*} *What does this word mean to you?*

{*Evening*} *What does this word mean to you?*

Meaning:

Sentence:

MONDAY JUNE 13TH

Famelicose ~ constantly hungry
FAM - EL - I - COSE

{Morning} What does this word mean to you?

{Evening} What does this word mean to you?

Meaning:

Sentence:

TUESDAY JUNE 14TH

Chrestomathic ~ of, or related to useful knowledge or learning
CRES - TO - MATH - IC

{*Morning*} *What does this word mean to you?*

{*Evening*} *What does this word mean to you?*

Meaning:

Sentence:

Wednesday June 15th

Nescience ~ the state of not knowing; ignorance
NES - EE - ENCE

{Morning} What does this word mean to you?

{Evening} What does this word mean to you?

Meaning:

Sentence:

Thursday June 16th

Logodaedalus ~ *a person who uses words with skill*
LOG - OH - DAY - DAL - US

{Morning} What does this word mean to you?

{Evening} What does this word mean to you?

Meaning:

Sentence:

Friday June 17th

Hodiernal ~ *of or relating to the present day*
HO - DEE - ER - NAL

{Morning} What does this word mean to you?

{Evening} What does this word mean to you?

Meaning:

Sentence:

SATURDAY JUNE 18TH

Yonderly ~ absent or distant minded
YON - DER - LEE

{Morning} What does this word mean to you?

{Evening} What does this word mean to you?

Meaning:

Sentence:

SUNDAY JUNE 19TH

Wistly ~ to do something with intent
WIST - LEE

{Morning} What does this word mean to you?

{Evening} What does this word mean to you?

Meaning:

Sentence:

Monday June 20th

Doctiloquent ~ to speak in a learned or educated manner
DOC - TIL - O - QUENT

{Morning} What does this word mean to you?

{Evening} What does this word mean to you?

Meaning:

Sentence:

TUESDAY JUNE 21ST

Semestral ~ occurring every six months
SEM - ES - TRAL

{*Morning*} *What does this word mean to you?*

{*Evening*} *What does this word mean to you?*

Meaning:

Sentence:

WEDNESDAY JUNE 22ND

Mendaciloquence ~ untruthful speech; lying
MEN - DA - CIL - O - QUENCE

{*Morning*} *What does this word mean to you?*

{*Evening*} *What does this word mean to you?*

Meaning:

Sentence:

Unicity ~ the quality of being unique; being united as a whole
U - NI - CI - TY

{*Morning*} *What does this word mean to you?*

{*Evening*} *What does this word mean to you?*

Meaning:

Sentence:

FRIDAY JUNE 24TH

Epeolatry ~ the worship of words
EP - EE - O - LA - TREE

{*Morning*} *What does this word mean to you?*

{*Evening*} *What does this word mean to you?*

Meaning:

Sentence:

SATURDAY JUNE 25TH

Arborize ~ *to branch out freely and repeatedly*
AR - BOR - IZE

{Morning} What does this word mean to you?

{Evening} What does this word mean to you?

Meaning:

Sentence:

Viaggiatory ~ travelling frequently
VI - AG - GI - A - TORY

{Morning} What does this word mean to you?

{Evening} What does this word mean to you?

Meaning:

Sentence:

Perseity ~ *a state of being that does not depend upon anything else* PER - SEE - IT - EE

{Morning} What does this word mean to you?

{Evening} What does this word mean to you?

Meaning:

Sentence:

TUESDAY JUNE 28TH

Ombrophobia ~ the fear of rain
OM - BRO - PHO - BEE - AH

{Morning} What does this word mean to you?

{Evening} What does this word mean to you?

Meaning:

Sentence:

WEDNESDAY JUNE 29TH

Thanatophobia ~ *the fear of death*
THA - NAT - O - PHO - BEE - AH

{*Morning*} *What does this word mean to you?*

{*Evening*} *What does this word mean to you?*

Meaning:

Sentence:

Thursday June 30th

Xenoglossia ~ phenomenon where one can speak and write a language they have not acquired naturally ZEE - NO - GLOSIA

{Morning} What does this word mean to you?

{Evening} What does this word mean to you?

Meaning:

Sentence:

FRIDAY JULY 1ST

Sophomania ~ *a delusion of superior intelligence*
SOP - O - MANIA

{Morning} *What does this word mean to you?*

{Evening} *What does this word mean to you?*

Meaning:

Sentence:

SATURDAY JULY 2ND

Quixotic ~ extremely idealistic in an impractical or unrealistic way

QUIX - OT - IC

{Morning} What does this word mean to you?

{Evening} What does this word mean to you?

Meaning:

Sentence:

Sunday July 3rd

Nexility ~ compactness of speech; using little words
NEX - IL - IT - EE

{*Morning*} *What does this word mean to you?*

{*Evening*} *What does this word mean to you?*

Meaning:

Sentence:

MONDAY JULY 4TH

Eleutherian ~ freedom giving
EE - LOO - THEE - REE - AN

{Morning} What does this word mean to you?

{Evening} What does this word mean to you?

Meaning:

Sentence:

Tuesday July 5th

Inaniloquent ~ *talking without sense*
IN - AN - IL - O - QUENT

{Morning} What does this word mean to you?

{Evening} What does this word mean to you?

Meaning:

Sentence:

WEDNESDAY JULY 6TH

Clinomania ~ *an excessive desire to stay in bed*
CLIN - O - MAY - NEE - AH

{*Morning*} *What does this word mean to you?*

{*Evening*} *What does this word mean to you?*

Meaning:

Sentence:

Thursday July 7th

Forisfamiliate ~ *to be free from parental authority*
FOR - ISS - FAM - IL - EE - ATE

{Morning} What does this word mean to you?

{Evening} What does this word mean to you?

Meaning:

Sentence:

FRIDAY JULY 8TH

Mentatiferous ~ telepathic; communicating thoughts without the use of senses

MEN - TAT - I - FER - US

{*Morning*} *What does this word mean to you?*

{*Evening*} *What does this word mean to you?*

Meaning:

Sentence:

Brumal ~ of or relating to winter
BREW - MUL

{Morning} What does this word mean to you?

{Evening} What does this word mean to you?

Meaning:

Sentence:

Doromania ~ an urge or desire to give gifts

DOOR - O - MANIA

{Morning} What does this word mean to you?

{Evening} What does this word mean to you?

Meaning:

Sentence:

Holobenthic ~ inhabiting the deep sea for all of life
HO - LO - BEN - THIC

{Morning} What does this word mean to you?

{Evening} What does this word mean to you?

Meaning:

Sentence:

Tuesday July 12th

Pertinacity ~ *adhering absolutely to a purpose or opinion*
PER - TIN - A - CITY

{Morning} What does this word mean to you?

{Evening} What does this word mean to you?

Meaning:

Sentence:

WEDNESDAY JULY 13TH

Theopneustic ~ inspired by a god

THEO - PUN - OO - STIC

{*Morning*} *What does this word mean to you?*

{*Evening*} *What does this word mean to you?*

Meaning:

Sentence:

Thursday July 14th

Equipollent ~ *equal in power or significance*

EQUIP - OL - LENT

{*Morning*} *What does this word mean to you?*

_____

_____

_____

_____

_____

_____

{*Evening*} *What does this word mean to you?*

_____

_____

_____

_____

_____

_____

Meaning:

_____

Sentence:

_____

_____

Friday July 15th

Unzymotic ~ fabulous
UN - ZY - MOT - IC

{Morning} What does this word mean to you?

{Evening} What does this word mean to you?

Meaning:

Sentence:

SATURDAY JULY 16TH

Worksome ~ hard working; industrious
WORK - SOME

{*Morning*} *What does this word mean to you?*

{*Evening*} *What does this word mean to you?*

Meaning:

Sentence:

Sunday July 17th

Ambulomancy ~ divination by walking; foretelling the future by walking

AM - BU - LO - MAN - SEE

{*Morning*} *What does this word mean to you?*

{*Evening*} *What does this word mean to you?*

Meaning:

Sentence:

MONDAY JULY 18TH

Omnicompetent ~ *able to deal with all matters*
OM - NEE - COM - PO - TENT

{*Morning*} *What does this word mean to you?*

{*Evening*} *What does this word mean to you?*

Meaning:

Sentence:

Tuesday July 19th

Sophrosyne ~ excellence of character; soundness of mind
SOPH - RO - SYNE

{*Morning*} *What does this word mean to you?*

{*Evening*} *What does this word mean to you?*

Meaning:

Sentence:

WEDNESDAY JULY 20TH

Gerascophobia ~ a fear of aging or growing old
GER - ASS - CO - PHO - BEE - AH

{*Morning*} *What does this word mean to you?*

{*Evening*} *What does this word mean to you?*

Meaning:

Sentence:

Nimiety ~ *more than is necessary; excessive*

NIM - IT - EE

{*Morning*} *What does this word mean to you?*

{*Evening*} *What does this word mean to you?*

Meaning:

Sentence:

FRIDAY JULY 22ND

Retrophilia ~ a strong love for the past or things of the past
RE - TRO - PHEE - LEE - AH

{*Morning*} *What does this word mean to you?*

{*Evening*} *What does this word mean to you?*

Meaning:

Sentence:

Viaticum ~ a provision or allowance for travelling; travel fund

VI - AT - I - CUM

{*Morning*} *What does this word mean to you?*

{*Evening*} *What does this word mean to you?*

Meaning:

Sentence:

SUNDAY JULY 24TH

Mercedary ~ an employer; one who hires
MER - CE - DARY

{Morning} What does this word mean to you?

{Evening} What does this word mean to you?

Meaning:

Sentence:

Monday July 25th

Longanimity ~ patient endurance of hardship; forbearance
LONG - AN - IM - IT - EE

{Morning} What does this word mean to you?

{Evening} What does this word mean to you?

Meaning:

Sentence:

Tirocinium ~ *early training or experience*
TIE - RO - SIN - EE - UM

{*Morning*} *What does this word mean to you?*

{*Evening*} *What does this word mean to you?*

Meaning:

Sentence:

Philalethist ~ a lover of truth
PHIL - AL - E - THIST

{*Morning*} *What does this word mean to you?*

{*Evening*} *What does this word mean to you?*

Meaning:

Sentence:

Thursday July 28th

Confelicity ~ delight or pleasure in someone else's happiness
CON - FEL - I - CIT - EE

{Morning} What does this word mean to you?

{Evening} What does this word mean to you?

Meaning:

Sentence:

FRIDAY JULY 29TH

Indigence ~ a state of extreme poverty

IN - DI - GENCE

{Morning} *What does this word mean to you?*

{Evening} *What does this word mean to you?*

Meaning:

Sentence:

Saturday July 30th

Drapetomania ~ an urge to run away
DRAPE - TOE - MANIA

{Morning} *What does this word mean to you?*

{Evening} *What does this word mean to you?*

Meaning:

Sentence:

Epigamic ~ attracting the opposite sex
EP - I - GAM - IC

{*Morning*} *What does this word mean to you?*

{*Evening*} *What does this word mean to you?*

Meaning:

Sentence:

MONDAY AUGUST 1ST

Titivate ~ *to make enhancements to; to smarten up*
TIT - I - VATE

{*Morning*} *What does this word mean to you?*

{*Evening*} *What does this word mean to you?*

Meaning:

Sentence:

TUESDAY AUGUST 2ND

Upaithric ~ open to the sky; without a roof or ceiling
U - PAY - THRIC

{*Morning*} *What does this word mean to you?*

{*Evening*} *What does this word mean to you?*

Meaning:

Sentence:

WEDNESDAY AUGUST 3RD

Ergasiomania ~ *an obsessive desire to work*
ERG - ASIO - MANIA

{*Morning*} *What does this word mean to you?*

{*Evening*} *What does this word mean to you?*

Meaning:

Sentence:

THURSDAY AUGUST 4TH

Holophrasis ~ the expression of a complex idea using one word

HO - LO - FRAY - SIS

{*Morning*} *What does this word mean to you?*

{*Evening*} *What does this word mean to you?*

Meaning:

Sentence:

FRIDAY AUGUST 5TH

Splenitive ~ fiery; passionate
SPLEN - IT - IVE

{Morning} What does this word mean to you?

{Evening} What does this word mean to you?

Meaning:

Sentence:

SATURDAY AUGUST 6TH

Vindictivolence ~ the desire to take revenge for oneself
VIN - DIC - TIV - O - LENCE

{Morning} What does this word mean to you?

{Evening} What does this word mean to you?

Meaning:

Sentence:

Sunday August 7th

Oniomania ~ an obsession with or impulse for buying things
ON - IO - MANIA

{Morning} What does this word mean to you?

{Evening} What does this word mean to you?

Meaning:

Sentence:

Monday August 8th

Abyssopelagic ~ referring to the deepest depths of the ocean
AB - ISS - O - PEL - A - GIC

{Morning} *What does this word mean to you?*

{Evening} *What does this word mean to you?*

Meaning:

Sentence:

TUESDAY AUGUST 9TH

Noctivagant ~ wandering in the night
NOC - TI - VAY - JANT

{Morning} What does this word mean to you?

{Evening} What does this word mean to you?

Meaning:

Sentence:

WEDNESDAY AUGUST 10TH

Gloaming ~ twilight; dusk; becoming dark;sunset
GLOW - MING

{Morning} What does this word mean to you?

{Evening} What does this word mean to you?

Meaning:

Sentence:

Thursday August 11th

Philomath ~ a lover of learning and studying
PHIL - O - MATH

{Morning} What does this word mean to you?

{Evening} What does this word mean to you?

Meaning:

Sentence:

FRIDAY AUGUST 12TH

Kenophobia ~ a fear of empty spaces
KEN - O - PHOBIA

{Morning} What does this word mean to you?

{Evening} What does this word mean to you?

Meaning:

Sentence:

Crescive ~ increasing; growing; gradual spontaneous development
CRES - CIVE

{Morning} What does this word mean to you?

{Evening} What does this word mean to you?

Meaning:

Sentence:

Metagnostic ~ beyond understanding and knowledge
MET - AG - NOS - TIC

{*Morning*} *What does this word mean to you?*

{*Evening*} *What does this word mean to you?*

Meaning:

Sentence:

MONDAY AUGUST 15TH

Lucripetous ~ *eager for gain*
LU - CRI - PET - OUS

{Morning} What does this word mean to you?

{Evening} What does this word mean to you?

Meaning:

Sentence:

Tuesday August 16th

Quomodocunquize ~ *to make money in any way possible*
QUO - MODO - CUN - QUIZE

{Morning} What does this word mean to you?

{Evening} What does this word mean to you?

Meaning:

Sentence:

Wednesday August 17th

Serendipity ~ *making desirable or happy discoveries by accident*

SER - EN - DIP - IT - EE

{*Morning*} *What does this word mean to you?*

_____

_____

_____

_____

_____

_____

_____

{*Evening*} *What does this word mean to you?*

_____

_____

_____

_____

_____

_____

_____

Meaning:

_____

_____

Sentence:

_____

_____

_____

THURSDAY AUGUST 18TH

Dromomania ~ an impulse or desire to wander or travel
DROM - O - MANIA

{Morning} What does this word mean to you?

{Evening} What does this word mean to you?

Meaning:

Sentence:

Friday August 19th

Constructivism ~ an approach to education allowing students to construct their own knowledge
CON - STRUCT - IV - ISM

{*Morning*} *What does this word mean to you?*

{*Evening*} *What does this word mean to you?*

Meaning:

Sentence:

Saturday August 20th

Jocoserious ~ *to be serious and joking at the same time*
JOC - O - SER - I - OUS

{*Morning*} *What does this word mean to you?*

{*Evening*} *What does this word mean to you?*

Meaning:

Sentence:

Sunday August 21st

Indwell ~ to be permanently present in someone's mind or soul
IN - DWELL

{Morning} What does this word mean to you?

{Evening} What does this word mean to you?

Meaning:

Sentence:

Erythrophobia ~ a fear of blushing
ER - EE - THRO - PHO - BEE - AH

{Morning} *What does this word mean to you?*

{Evening} *What does this word mean to you?*

Meaning:

Sentence:

TUESDAY AUGUST 23RD

Bailiwick ~ a person's area of skill, expertise or interests
BAIL - I - WICK

{*Morning*} *What does this word mean to you?*

{*Evening*} *What does this word mean to you?*

Meaning:

Sentence:

Wednesday August 24th

Forswink ~ *to exhaust through toil*
FORCE - WINK

{Morning} What does this word mean to you?

{Evening} What does this word mean to you?

Meaning:

Sentence:

Thursday August 25th

Phrontistery ~ *a thinking place; a school or educational place*
PRONE - TIST - ER - EE

{*Morning*} *What does this word mean to you?*

{*Evening*} *What does this word mean to you?*

Meaning:

Sentence:

Ontocyclic ~ returning to a youthful state of character at an old age

ON - TOE - CYC - LIC

{*Morning*} *What does this word mean to you?*

{*Evening*} *What does this word mean to you?*

Meaning:

Sentence:

SATURDAY AUGUST 27TH

Nolition ~ unwillingness to do something
NO - LISH - ON

{*Morning*} *What does this word mean to you?*

{*Evening*} *What does this word mean to you?*

Meaning:

Sentence:

Horripilation ~ hairs on your arms standing up due to excitement or fear

HO - RIP - IL - AY - SHUN

{Morning} What does this word mean to you?

{Evening} What does this word mean to you?

Meaning:

Sentence:

MONDAY AUGUST 29TH

Misocainea ~ hatred of new ideas
MIS - O - CAIN - EE - AH

{Morning} What does this word mean to you?

{Evening} What does this word mean to you?

Meaning:

Sentence:

TUESDAY AUGUST 30TH

Aeipathy ~ *an enduring and consuming passion*
EE - PATH - EE

{*Morning*} *What does this word mean to you?*

{*Evening*} *What does this word mean to you?*

Meaning:

Sentence:

WEDNESDAY AUGUST 31ST

Tolutiloquence ~ smooth or flowing speech
TOL - U - TIL - O - QUENCE

{*Morning*} *What does this word mean to you?*

_____

_____

_____

_____

_____

_____

_____

{*Evening*} *What does this word mean to you?*

_____

_____

_____

_____

_____

_____

_____

Meaning:

_____

_____

Sentence:

_____

_____

_____

Thursday September 1st

Xenophilia ~ a love for foreign people, customs or cultures
ZEE - NO - FEE - LEE - AH

{Morning} What does this word mean to you?

{Evening} What does this word mean to you?

Meaning:

Sentence:

FRIDAY SEPTEMBER 2ND

Tonitrophobia ~ a fear of thunder and lightning
TOE - NI - TRO - PHO - BEE - AH

{*Morning*} *What does this word mean to you?*

{*Evening*} *What does this word mean to you?*

Meaning:

Sentence:

Stultiloquence ~ senseless or foolish talk
STUL - TIL - O - QUENCE

{*Morning*} *What does this word mean to you?*

_____
_____
_____
_____
_____
_____
_____

{*Evening*} *What does this word mean to you?*

_____
_____
_____
_____
_____
_____

Meaning:

_____
_____

Sentence:

_____
_____

Visceral ~ relating to deep internal feelings; instinctive
VIS - CER - AL

{*Morning*} *What does this word mean to you?*

{*Evening*} *What does this word mean to you?*

Meaning:

Sentence:

MONDAY SEPTEMBER 5TH

Rhathymia ~ the state of being care free; light hearted
RHA - THY - ME - AH

{*Morning*} *What does this word mean to you?*

{*Evening*} *What does this word mean to you?*

Meaning:

Sentence:

Zoetic ~ of and relating to life and living; vital
ZO - ET - IC

{Morning} What does this word mean to you?

{Evening} What does this word mean to you?

Meaning:

Sentence:

WEDNESDAY SEPTEMBER 7TH

Dulcifluous ~ flowing sweetly, in a gentle manner
DUL - CI - FLEW - US

{Morning} What does this word mean to you?

{Evening} What does this word mean to you?

Meaning:

Sentence:

THURSDAY SEPTEMBER 8TH

Yeasty ~ youthful; creative; restless
YEAST - EE

{Morning} What does this word mean to you?

{Evening} What does this word mean to you?

Meaning:

Sentence:

FRIDAY SEPTEMBER 9TH

Plerophory ~ a state of full confidence; absolute certainty
PLE - RO - FOR - EE

{Morning} What does this word mean to you?

{Evening} What does this word mean to you?

Meaning:

Sentence:

Counterphobic ~ seeking out what one fears in an attempt to overcome that fear

COUNT - ER - PHO - BIC

{Morning} What does this word mean to you?

{Evening} What does this word mean to you?

Meaning:

Sentence:

Ethnomania ~ an obsessive devotion to one's own people
ETH - NO - MAY - NEE - AH

{*Morning*} *What does this word mean to you?*

{*Evening*} *What does this word mean to you?*

Meaning:

Sentence:

Writative ~ inclined to write a lot; addicted to writing
WRIT - AT - IVE

{Morning} What does this word mean to you?

{Evening} What does this word mean to you?

Meaning:

Sentence:

TUESDAY SEPTEMBER 13TH

Misosophy ~ a hatred of wisdom and knowledge
MIS - O - SOPH - EE

{Morning} What does this word mean to you?

{Evening} What does this word mean to you?

Meaning:

Sentence:

Interramificiation ~ the union of branches to form a network
IN - TER - RAM - I - FI - CAY - SHUN

{*Morning*} *What does this word mean to you?*

{*Evening*} *What does this word mean to you?*

Meaning:

Sentence:

THURSDAY SEPTEMBER 15TH

Ludibund ~ playful; sportful
LUD - I - BUND

{*Morning*} *What does this word mean to you?*

{*Evening*} *What does this word mean to you?*

Meaning:

Sentence:

FRIDAY SEPTEMBER 16TH

Nostomania ~ *a desire to return home; homesickness*
NOS - TO - MAY - NEE - AH

{*Morning*} *What does this word mean to you?*

{*Evening*} *What does this word mean to you?*

Meaning:

Sentence:

Saturday September 17th

Fritiniency ~ *the noise of insects*
FRIT - IN - EE - EN - SEE

{Morning} What does this word mean to you?

{Evening} What does this word mean to you?

Meaning:

Sentence:

SUNDAY SEPTEMBER 18TH

Opsimath ~ a person who continues to learn and study late in life

OP - SI - MATH

{*Morning*} *What does this word mean to you?*

{*Evening*} *What does this word mean to you?*

Meaning:

Sentence:

Uranomania ~ obsession with the idea of divinity; a belief that one comes from divine origins
UR - AN - O - MANIA

{*Morning*} *What does this word mean to you?*

{*Evening*} *What does this word mean to you?*

Meaning:

Sentence:

Viscerotonic ~ sociable, easygoing; comfort seeking
VISS - ER - O - TON - IC

{*Morning*} *What does this word mean to you?*

{*Evening*} *What does this word mean to you?*

Meaning:

Sentence:

Amarulence ~ *bitterness; anger and disappointment at being treated unfairly*

AM - AR - U - LENCE

{Morning} What does this word mean to you?

{Evening} What does this word mean to you?

Meaning:

Sentence:

Humanitarianism ~ an active belief in the value of human life

HU - MAN - I - TARE - EE - AN - ISM

{Morning} What does this word mean to you?

{Evening} What does this word mean to you?

Meaning:

Sentence:

Goluptious ~ addicted to sensual indulgences or luxurious pleasures; delightful
GOL - UP - SHUS

{*Morning*} *What does this word mean to you?*

{*Evening*} *What does this word mean to you?*

Meaning:

Sentence:

Plutolatry ~ an excessive devotion to wealth
PLU - TOE - LA - TREE

{*Morning*} *What does this word mean to you?*

{*Evening*} *What does this word mean to you?*

Meaning:

Sentence:

Yagiment ~ a state of excitement
YA - GI - MENT

{Morning} What does this word mean to you?

{Evening} What does this word mean to you?

Meaning:

Sentence:

MONDAY SEPTEMBER 26TH

Suaveolent ~ fragrant or sweet smelling
SWA - VO - LENT

{*Morning*} *What does this word mean to you?*

{*Evening*} *What does this word mean to you?*

Meaning:

Sentence:

TUESDAY SEPTEMBER 27TH

Desultory ~ lacking a plan, purpose or enthusiasm
DES - UL - TOR - EE

{*Morning*} *What does this word mean to you?*

{*Evening*} *What does this word mean to you?*

Meaning:

Sentence:

Topiary ~ the art of clipping trees or bushes into shapes
TOP - EE - ARY

{Morning} What does this word mean to you?

{Evening} What does this word mean to you?

Meaning:

Sentence:

Thursday September 29th

Multiloquent ~ speaking much; talkative
MUL - TIL - O - QUENT

{*Morning*} *What does this word mean to you?*

_____

_____

_____

_____

_____

_____

{*Evening*} *What does this word mean to you?*

_____

_____

_____

_____

_____

_____

Meaning:

_____

Sentence:

_____

_____

FRIDAY SEPTEMBER 30TH

Quotennial ~ occurring yearly; annual
QWO - TEE - NEE - AL

{*Morning*} *What does this word mean to you?*

{*Evening*} *What does this word mean to you?*

Meaning:

Sentence:

SATURDAY OCTOBER 1ST

*Eucatastrophe ~ a sudden and favorable resolution of events;
a happy ending*
EU - CAT - AS - TRO - PHEE

{*Morning*} *What does this word mean to you?*

{*Evening*} *What does this word mean to you?*

Meaning:

Sentence:

SUNDAY OCTOBER 2ND

Cursorial ~ having limbs adapted for running
CUR - SORE - EE - AL

{*Morning*} *What does this word mean to you?*

{*Evening*} *What does this word mean to you?*

Meaning:

Sentence:

Subnubilar ~ *located under the clouds*

SUB - NUB - IL - AR

{Morning} What does this word mean to you?

{Evening} What does this word mean to you?

Meaning:

Sentence:

TUESDAY OCTOBER 4TH

Nullifidian ~ a person with no faith or belief
NULL - I - FID - EE - AN

{*Morning*} *What does this word mean to you?*

{*Evening*} *What does this word mean to you?*

Meaning:

Sentence:

Poriomania ~ an irresistible desire to journey away from home
POR - EE - O - MANIA

{Morning} What does this word mean to you?

{Evening} What does this word mean to you?

Meaning:

Sentence:

Lynchnobite ~ *one who works at night and sleeps during the day*

LINCH - NO - BITE

{Morning} *What does this word mean to you?*

{Evening} *What does this word mean to you?*

Meaning:

Sentence:

Boscaresque ~ picturesque; beautiful like a forest
BOS - CAR - ESS - CK

{Morning} What does this word mean to you?

{Evening} What does this word mean to you?

Meaning:

Sentence:

SATURDAY OCTOBER 8TH

Gradation ~ *a change taking place through a series of stages*
GRAY - DAY - SHUN

{*Morning*} *What does this word mean to you?*

{*Evening*} *What does this word mean to you?*

Meaning:

Sentence:

Intersidereal ~ situated amongst the stars; interstellar
IN - TER - SIDE - EER - EE - AL

{*Morning*} *What does this word mean to you?*

{*Evening*} *What does this word mean to you?*

Meaning:

Sentence:

Topophilia ~ a strong sense of place; the love of or a strong connection with a place

TOP - O - PHIL - EE - AH

{*Morning*} *What does this word mean to you?*

{*Evening*} *What does this word mean to you?*

Meaning:

Sentence:

Funambulism ~ tightrope walking; a show of mental agility
FUN - AM - BU - LISM

{*Morning*} *What does this word mean to you?*

{*Evening*} *What does this word mean to you?*

Meaning:

Sentence:

WEDNESDAY OCTOBER 12TH

Oragious ~ stormy; tempestuous
OR - A - GI - OUS

{Morning} What does this word mean to you?

{Evening} What does this word mean to you?

Meaning:

Sentence:

Thursday October 13th

Amorevolous ~ loving; kind; charitable
AM - OR - E - VOL - OUS

{Morning} What does this word mean to you?

{Evening} What does this word mean to you?

Meaning:

Sentence:

Vivisepulture ~ the practice of burying someone alive
VIV - I - SEP - UL - TURE

{*Morning*} *What does this word mean to you?*

{*Evening*} *What does this word mean to you?*

Meaning:

Sentence:

Multipotent ~ extremely powerful; having the power to do many things

MUL - TI - PO - TENT

{*Morning*} *What does this word mean to you?*

{*Evening*} *What does this word mean to you?*

Meaning:

Sentence:

Hyetal ~ of or relating to rain or rainfall
HIGH - EE - TAL

{*Morning*} *What does this word mean to you?*

{*Evening*} *What does this word mean to you?*

Meaning:

Sentence:

Doughty ~ brave and persistent; fearless
DOW - TEE

{*Morning*} *What does this word mean to you?*

{*Evening*} *What does this word mean to you?*

Meaning:

Sentence:

TUESDAY OCTOBER 18TH

Xenophobia ~ fear and hatred of anything strange or foreign
ZEN - O - PHO - BEE - AH

{*Morning*} *What does this word mean to you?*

{*Evening*} *What does this word mean to you?*

Meaning:

Sentence:

WEDNESDAY OCTOBER 19TH

Redamancy ~ the act of loving in return
RED - A - MAN - SEE

{*Morning*} *What does this word mean to you?*

{*Evening*} *What does this word mean to you?*

Meaning:

Sentence:

THURSDAY OCTOBER 20TH

Procellous ~ stormy
PRO - CELL - OUS

{*Morning*} *What does this word mean to you?*

{*Evening*} *What does this word mean to you?*

Meaning:

Sentence:

Eupraxia ~ good conduct; the personification of well-being; ability to perform muscle movement
YOU - PRAX - EE - AH

{*Morning*} *What does this word mean to you?*

{*Evening*} *What does this word mean to you?*

Meaning:

Sentence:

SATURDAY OCTOBER 22ND

Nummamorous ~ money loving .
NUMM - AM - OR - OUS

{*Morning*} *What does this word mean to you?*

{*Evening*} *What does this word mean to you?*

Meaning:

Sentence:

Klendusic ~ resistant to disease or infection
KLEN - DUE - SIC

{Morning} What does this word mean to you?

{Evening} What does this word mean to you?

Meaning:

Sentence:

MONDAY OCTOBER 24TH

Cynosure ~ a person or thing at the centre of attention owing to brilliance

CYN - O - SURE

{Morning} *What does this word mean to you?*

{Evening} *What does this word mean to you?*

Meaning:

Sentence:

Tuesday October 25th

Uranophobia ~ *a fear of heaven or the sky*
UR - AN - O - PHO - BEE - AH

{Morning} What does this word mean to you?

{Evening} What does this word mean to you?

Meaning:

Sentence:

Supercilious ~ behaving as though one is superior to others
SU - PER - CIL - EE - OUS

{*Morning*} *What does this word mean to you?*

{*Evening*} *What does this word mean to you?*

Meaning:

Sentence:

Lyterian ~ terminating a disease; indicating the end of a disease

LIE - TEAR - EE - AN

{*Morning*} *What does this word mean to you?*

{*Evening*} *What does this word mean to you?*

Meaning:

Sentence:

FRIDAY OCTOBER 28TH

Orarian ~ a person who lives on the coast; coastal
OR - AIR - EE - AN

{*Morning*} *What does this word mean to you?*

{*Evening*} *What does this word mean to you?*

Meaning:

Sentence:

Debouch ~ *to emerge from a confined space into an open area*
DEE - BOUCH

{*Morning*} *What does this word mean to you?*

{*Evening*} *What does this word mean to you?*

Meaning:

Sentence:

SUNDAY OCTOBER 30TH

Volitient ~ *brought about by free will; voluntary*
VOL - I - TEE - ENT

{*Morning*} *What does this word mean to you?*

{*Evening*} *What does this word mean to you?*

Meaning:

Sentence:

Munificent ~ characterized by giving; generosity
MU - NI - FI - CENT

{Morning} What does this word mean to you?

{Evening} What does this word mean to you?

Meaning:

Sentence:

TUESDAY NOVEMBER 1ST

Juvenescent ~ youthful; the state of being young
JU - VE - NES - CENT

{*Morning*} *What does this word mean to you?*

{*Evening*} *What does this word mean to you?*

Meaning:

Sentence:

Ipseity ~ individual identity; the quality of being oneself
IP - SAY - IT - EE

{*Morning*} *What does this word mean to you?*

{*Evening*} *What does this word mean to you?*

Meaning:

Sentence:

THURSDAY NOVEMBER 3RD

Flavescent ~ something that is yellow; turning yellow
FLAV - ES - CENT

{*Morning*} *What does this word mean to you?*

{*Evening*} *What does this word mean to you?*

Meaning:

Sentence:

FRIDAY NOVEMBER 4TH

Apricity ~ the warmth of the sun in Winter
A - PRI - CI - TEE

{Morning} *What does this word mean to you?*

{Evening} *What does this word mean to you?*

Meaning:

Sentence:

SATURDAY NOVEMBER 5TH

Orthobiosis ~ the correct way of living; right living
OR - THO - BI - O - SIS

{*Morning*} *What does this word mean to you?*

{*Evening*} *What does this word mean to you?*

Meaning:

Sentence:

Dichotomy ~ a division into two parts; a contrast between two things DI - COT - O - ME

{Morning} What does this word mean to you?

{Evening} What does this word mean to you?

Meaning:

Sentence:

MONDAY NOVEMBER 7TH

Prospice ~ to look forward
PROS - PICE

{Morning} What does this word mean to you?

{Evening} What does this word mean to you?

Meaning:

Sentence:

Tuesday November 8th

Nycthemeron ~ a full period of 24 hours including day and night

NYC - THE - MER - ON

{Morning} What does this word mean to you?

{Evening} What does this word mean to you?

Meaning:

Sentence:

WEDNESDAY NOVEMBER 9TH

Hyperbulia ~ the possession of great will force
HY - PER - BU - LEE - AH

{*Morning*} *What does this word mean to you?*

{*Evening*} *What does this word mean to you?*

Meaning:

Sentence:

Eupsychics ~ proper education to induce human progress
EU - SIGH - KICKS

{*Morning*} *What does this word mean to you?*

{*Evening*} *What does this word mean to you?*

Meaning:

Sentence:

Friday November 11th

Translunary ~ *located beyond or above the moon*
TRANS - LU - NAR - EE

{Morning} *What does this word mean to you?*

{Evening} *What does this word mean to you?*

Meaning:

Sentence:

Urbicolous ~ *of or relating to a city*

UR - BI - COL - OUS

{Morning} What does this word mean to you?

{Evening} What does this word mean to you?

Meaning:

Sentence:

SUNDAY NOVEMBER 13TH

Supererogation ~ doing more than what is asked
SU - PER - ER - O - GA - TION

{*Morning*} *What does this word mean to you?*

{*Evening*} *What does this word mean to you?*

Meaning:

Sentence:

Quotidian ~ occurring daily
QUO - TID - I - AN

{*Morning*} *What does this word mean to you?*

{*Evening*} *What does this word mean to you?*

Meaning:

Sentence:

Cosmognosis ~ the natural instinct that tells creatures when to migrate COS - MO - NO - SIS

{*Morning*} *What does this word mean to you?*

{*Evening*} *What does this word mean to you?*

Meaning:

Sentence:

Moonglade ~ the bright reflection of moonlight on water
MOON - GLADE

{*Morning*} *What does this word mean to you?*

{*Evening*} *What does this word mean to you?*

Meaning:

Sentence:

Thursday November 17th

Locupletative ~ tending to enrich and improve
LOC - U - PLE - TATE - IVE

{*Morning*} *What does this word mean to you?*

{*Evening*} *What does this word mean to you?*

Meaning:

Sentence:

FRIDAY NOVEMBER 18TH

Voluble ~ *one who speaks easily and often; fluency of speech*
VOL - U - BUL

{*Morning*} *What does this word mean to you?*

{*Evening*} *What does this word mean to you?*

Meaning:

Sentence:

SATURDAY NOVEMBER 19TH

Transpicuous ~ *easily understood; transparent*
TRAN - SPIC - U - OUS

{*Morning*} *What does this word mean to you?*

{*Evening*} *What does this word mean to you?*

Meaning:

Sentence:

Zygnomic ~ a legally supported constraint on human freedom
ZIG - NOMIC

{*Morning*} *What does this word mean to you?*

{*Evening*} *What does this word mean to you?*

Meaning:

Sentence:

Breviloquent ~ concise speech or writing; using few words
BREV - IL -O - QUENT

{*Morning*} *What does this word mean to you?*

{*Evening*} *What does this word mean to you?*

Meaning:

Sentence:

Ostrichism ~ *the act of refusing to accept reality*

OS - TRICH - ISM

{*Morning*} *What does this word mean to you?*

{*Evening*} *What does this word mean to you?*

Meaning:

Sentence:

WEDNESDAY NOVEMBER 23RD

Gymnasiarchy ~ government over a school
GYM - NAY - SI - AR - KEY

{Morning} What does this word mean to you?

{Evening} What does this word mean to you?

Meaning:

Sentence:

Thursday November 24th

Nyctophobia ~ an extreme fear of night and darkness
NICK - TO - PHO - BEE - AH

{Morning} What does this word mean to you?

{Evening} What does this word mean to you?

Meaning:

Sentence:

FRIDAY NOVEMBER 25TH

Iracundulous ~ easily angered
IR - A - CUN - DUE - LOUS

{*Morning*} *What does this word mean to you?*

{*Evening*} *What does this word mean to you?*

Meaning:

Sentence:

Saturday November 26th

Apanthropinization ~ *the act of withdrawing oneself from society, humanity, or human concerns*

AP - AN - THROP - IN - IZATION

{*Morning*} *What does this word mean to you?*

{*Evening*} *What does this word mean to you?*

Meaning:

Sentence:

Doyen ~ the person with the most expertise in an area
DOY - EN

{Morning} What does this word mean to you?

{Evening} What does this word mean to you?

Meaning:

Sentence:

Felicity ~ intense happiness; the ability to find appropriate expression for one's thoughts
FEL - I - CIT - EE

{Morning} What does this word mean to you?

{Evening} What does this word mean to you?

Meaning:

Sentence:

TUESDAY NOVEMBER 29TH

Sybaritic ~ fond of sensuous luxury and pleasure; self indulgent
SIGH - BAR - IT - IC

{Morning} *What does this word mean to you?*

{Evening} *What does this word mean to you?*

Meaning:

Sentence:

Eximious ~ excellent; distinguished; chosen
EX - IM - EE - US

{*Morning*} *What does this word mean to you?*

{*Evening*} *What does this word mean to you?*

Meaning:

Sentence:

Triskaidekaphophobia ~ a fear of the number thirteen
TRIS - KAI - DE - KAPH - O - PHO - BIA

{*Morning*} What does this word mean to you?

{*Evening*} What does this word mean to you?

Meaning:

Sentence:

FRIDAY DECEMBER 2ND

Philargyrist ~ a lover of money
PHIL - AR - GY - RIST

{*Morning*} *What does this word mean to you?*

{*Evening*} *What does this word mean to you?*

Meaning:

Sentence:

SATURDAY DECEMBER 3RD

Hirquitalliency ~ the strength of a person's voice
HIR - QUIT - AY - LEE - EN - SEE

{*Morning*} *What does this word mean to you?*

{*Evening*} *What does this word mean to you?*

Meaning:

Sentence:

Rogalian ~ *of or relating to a great fire*
RO - GAY - LEE - AN

{Morning} What does this word mean to you?

{Evening} What does this word mean to you?

Meaning:

Sentence:

Monday December 5th

Utinam ~ a fervent wish or desire
U - TIN - AM

{*Morning*} *What does this word mean to you?*

{*Evening*} *What does this word mean to you?*

Meaning:

Sentence:

Tuesday December 6th

Psithurism ~ the sound of wind in the trees; the sound of the rustling of leaves
SITH - UR - ISM

{*Morning*} *What does this word mean to you?*

{*Evening*} *What does this word mean to you?*

Meaning:

Sentence:

WEDNESDAY DECEMBER 7TH

Contrivance ~ the use of skill to create something
CON - TRI - VANCE

{Morning} What does this word mean to you?

{Evening} What does this word mean to you?

Meaning:

Sentence:

Lubency ~ *willingness; pleasure*
LU - BEN - CY

{Morning} What does this word mean to you?

{Evening} What does this word mean to you?

Meaning:

Sentence:

FRIDAY DECEMBER 9TH

Punctiuncle ~ insignificant or trivial point of an argument
PUNCT - EE - UNCLE

{*Morning*} *What does this word mean to you?*

{*Evening*} *What does this word mean to you?*

Meaning:

Sentence:

Saturday December 10th

Mariturient ~ *eager to marry*
MAR - EE - TUR - EE - ENT

{*Morning*} *What does this word mean to you?*

{*Evening*} *What does this word mean to you?*

Meaning:

Sentence:

SUNDAY DECEMBER 11TH

Xenization ~ travelling alone in a foreign land
ZEN - I - ZAY - SHUN

{*Morning*} *What does this word mean to you?*

{*Evening*} *What does this word mean to you?*

Meaning:

Sentence:

Novaturient ~ desiring or seeking change in one's life
NO - VA - TUR - EE - ENT

{*Morning*} *What does this word mean to you?*

{*Evening*} *What does this word mean to you?*

Meaning:

Sentence:

Zoilist ~ an unnecessarily harsh critic
ZOY - LIST

{*Morning*} *What does this word mean to you?*

{*Evening*} *What does this word mean to you?*

Meaning:

Sentence:

Uxorious ~ fond of or submissive toward one's wife
UX - OR - I - OUS

{Morning} What does this word mean to you?

{Evening} What does this word mean to you?

Meaning:

Sentence:

Thursday December 15th

Weltschmerz ~ world weariness; a state of unhappiness with the world

VELT - SCHMERZ

{Morning} What does this word mean to you?

{Evening} What does this word mean to you?

Meaning:

Sentence:

Mnemonist ~ *a person with a great memory*
MNEM - ON - IST

{*Morning*} *What does this word mean to you?*

{*Evening*} *What does this word mean to you?*

Meaning:

Sentence:

Saturday December 17th

Impigrity ~ speed; quickness
IM - PIG - RIT - EE

{Morning} What does this word mean to you?

{Evening} What does this word mean to you?

Meaning:

Sentence:

Sunday December 18th

Algetic ~ relating to or causing pain
AL - JET - ICK

{*Morning*} *What does this word mean to you?*

{*Evening*} *What does this word mean to you?*

Meaning:

Sentence:

MONDAY DECEMBER 19TH

Expergefacient ~ something that is awakening or arousing
EX - PER - JE - FAY - SHENT

{Morning} What does this word mean to you?

{Evening} What does this word mean to you?

Meaning:

Sentence:

TUESDAY DECEMBER 20TH

Eirenism ~ a peaceful state of mind
AIR - E - NISM

{*Morning*} *What does this word mean to you?*

{*Evening*} *What does this word mean to you?*

Meaning:

Sentence:

WEDNESDAY DECEMBER 21ST

Fastidious ~ paying great attention to detail; meticulous
FAST - I - DEE - OUS

{*Morning*} *What does this word mean to you?*

{*Evening*} *What does this word mean to you?*

Meaning:

Sentence:

Pulchritude ~ beauty
PUL - CHRI - TUDE

{Morning} *What does this word mean to you?*

{Evening} *What does this word mean to you?*

Meaning:

Sentence:

FRIDAY DECEMBER 23RD

Satyagraha ~ passive political resistance; truth force
SAT - YAH - GRA - HA

{Morning} What does this word mean to you?

{Evening} What does this word mean to you?

Meaning:

Sentence:

Traboccant ~ excessive and abundant
TRA - BOCC - ANT

{Morning} *What does this word mean to you?*

{Evening} *What does this word mean to you?*

Meaning:

Sentence:

Zeal ~ great energy or enthusiasm in pursuit of something
ZEEL

{Morning} What does this word mean to you?

{Evening} What does this word mean to you?

Meaning:

Sentence:

Nascent ~ just coming into existence and displaying signs of future potential; developing
NAY - SCENT

{Morning} What does this word mean to you?

{Evening} What does this word mean to you?

Meaning:

Sentence:

TUESDAY DECEMBER 27TH

Hyemation ~ the passing of winter
HIGH - MAY - SHUN

{*Morning*} *What does this word mean to you?*

{*Evening*} *What does this word mean to you?*

Meaning:

Sentence:

Nubivagant ~ moving through air; wandering among the clouds

NEW - BE - VAY - JANT

{Morning} What does this word mean to you?

{Evening} What does this word mean to you?

Meaning:

Sentence:

Thursday December 29th

Gyniolatry ~ deep respect for and devotion to women
GUY - NEE - OL - A - TREE

{*Morning*} *What does this word mean to you?*

{*Evening*} *What does this word mean to you?*

Meaning:

Sentence:

Lodestar ~ a person or thing that serves as an inspiration or Guide

LODE - STAR

{Morning} What does this word mean to you?

{Evening} What does this word mean to you?

Meaning:

Sentence:

Patration ~ the completion or perfection of something
PAT - RAY - SHUN

{*Morning*} *What does this word mean to you?*

{*Evening*} *What does this word mean to you?*

Meaning:

Sentence:

Bibliography

BRM Institute, and Lindsey Horton. "The Neuroscience Behind Our words." *BRM.Institute*, 8th August 2019, *https://brm.institute/neuroscience-behind-words/*.

Chrisomalis, Stephen. "The Phrontistery." *The Phrontistery*, Stephen Chrisomalis, 1996, https://phrontistery.info/q.html.

Newberg, Andrew B., and Mark Robert Waldman. *Words Can Change Your Brain*. Penguin Publishing Group, 2013.
BRM. Institute, https://brm.institute/neuroscience-behind-words/.

Piercy, Joseph. *1000 Words to expand your vocabulary*. London, Michael O'Mara Books Limited, 2018.

Richter, Maria, et al. "Do Words Hurt? Brain activation during the processing of pain related words."
Science Direct, February 2010,
https://www.sciencedirect.com/science/article/abs/pii/S0304395909 004564.

Printed in Poland
by Amazon Fulfillment
Poland Sp. z o.o., Wrocław
12 March 2022

db74c4e5-1d37-46bf-8436-6f80ff2f3d7aR02